THE MAN IN THE CEILING

Book by Jules Feiffer
Based on his novel

Music and Lyrics by
Andrew Lippa

ISBN 978-1-5400-6043-3

HAL•LEONARD®

Visit Hal Leonard Online at
www.halleonard.com

Contact us:
Hal Leonard
7777 West Bluemound Road
Milwaukee, WI 53213
Email: info@halleonard.com

In Europe, contact:
Hal Leonard Europe Limited
42 Wigmore Street
Marylebone, London, W1U 2RN
Email: info@halleonardeurope.com

In Australia, contact:
Hal Leonard Australia Pty. Ltd.
4 Lentara Court
Cheltenham, Victoria, 3192 Australia
Email: info@halleonard.com.au

Jules Feiffer (book; original novel) is an award-winning cartoonist, playwright, screenwriter and children's book author, and illustrator. From his Village Voice editorial cartoons to his plays and screenplays (including *Little Murders and Carnal Knowledge*), Feiffer has been one of America's most prominent satirists for over fifty years. The first cartoonist commissioned by The New York Times to create comic strips for their Op-Ed page, Feiffer has since shifted his focus towards writing and illustrating books for children and young adults.

He won a Pulitzer Prize and a George Polk Award for his cartoons; an Obie for his plays; an Academy Award for the animation of his cartoon satire, *Munro*; and Lifetime Achievement Awards from the Writers Guild of America and the National Cartoonist Society. Feiffer has taught at the Yale School of Drama, Northwestern University, Dartmouth, and at Stony Brook Southampton College. He has been honored with major retrospectives at the New York Historical Society, the Library of Congress, and The School of Visual Arts. Presently, he is writing and illustrating graphic novels, beginning with his noir trilogy *Kill My Mother* (2014) and currently on a series of fantasy graphic novels for middle readers. He also does a monthly political cartoon for *Tablet*, an online magazine.

Andrew Lippa (music/lyrics) wrote and composed the theatrical oratorio *I Am Harvey Milk* that received its New York premiere at Lincoln Center starring Kristin Chenoweth and Mr. Lippa as Harvey Milk. *Life of the Party*, an evening celebrating 20 years of his work, premiered at London's award-winning Menier Chocolate Factory in 2014. He also wrote the Drama Desk-nominated music and lyrics for the Broadway musical Big Fish, the Tony-nominated music and lyrics for the Broadway musical *The Addams Family* (performed in over 40 countries; seen by over 30 million people worldwide) as well as the music for Aaron Sorkin's Broadway play *The Farnsworth Invention*. His song *Evil Like Me*, from Disney's *Descendants*, has been viewed over 70 million times on YouTube and earned Mr. Lippa his first gold record. Other musicals include the Drama Desk award-winning musical *The Wild Party* (book/music/lyrics); *A Little Princess* (music); *John & Jen* (music/book); *Asphalt Beach* (music and lyrics); and *You're A Good Man, Charlie Brown* (additional music/lyrics and arrangements). *Unbreakable*, a choral/theatrical work for men's chorus, soloists and orchestra tours the U.S. in 2019/2020 and is recorded on Ghostlight Records.

Accolades include a Tony and Grammy nomination, the Gilman/Gonzalez-Falla Theater Foundation Award, ASCAP's Richard Rodgers/New Horizons Award, The Drama Desk and The Outer Critics Circle Award. Andrew Lippa serves as President of the Dramatists Guild Foundation (dgf.org), is a graduate of The University of Michigan, and was born in Leeds, England. www.andrewlippa.com

Exclusive stage performing rights are represented by:
Theatrical Rights Worldwide, 1180 Avenue Of The Americas, Suite 640, New York, NY 10036
www.theatricalrights.com

CONTENTS

DOIN' FINE

Words and Music by
ANDREW LIPPA

Fun Jungle Feel ♩ = 88

Here in the jun - gle, filled_ with dan - gers, no - bo - dy knows_ which way_ to turn.__

Who in the jun - gle is___ your friend,_ and who in the end__ will watch_ you burn?_

Ev - 'ry-one out__ there wants_ to kill__ you, try-ing to eat__ your flesh_ and bone._

Who can you turn_ to in___ the jun - gle when you're feel - ing most_ a lone?_ Whose face will be a friend-ly

face? Who's gon-na get___ you through. this place?___ I'm your

pal, I'm your friend, I'm the one___just 'round_ the bend._ I will save you when your life is on the line._

___ I'm your guide, I'm your guy, I'm the on - ly rea - son why_ you will

Do what you can__ to keep__ on go - ing, do what you can__ with my__ ad - vice.__

And don't you e - ver think twice!__ So

kid-do, kid-do, kid-do, stick with me. And kid-do, kid-do, kid-do, you will

see_____ I'm your pal, I'm your friend, I'm your

ALMOST THERE

Words and Music by
ANDREW LIPPA

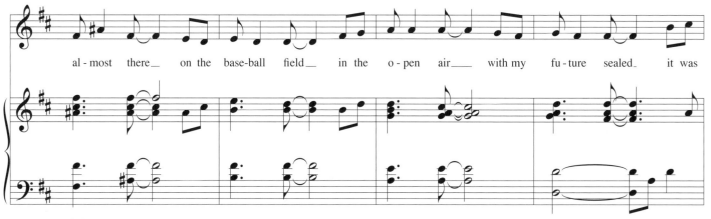

al - most there__ on the base-ball field__ in the o - pen air__ with my fu -ture sealed_ it was

Pedal OK

al - most real__ like a dream you feel__ when you wake up the mo - ment it's

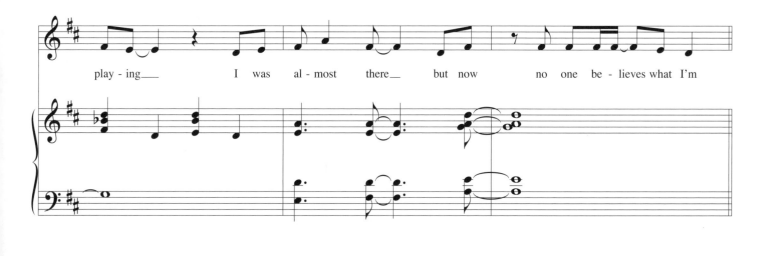

play - ing__ I was al - most there__ but now no one be - lieves what I'm

say-ing. That's wrong, my daugh-ter be-lieves how it was_

mf

No Pedal

and she's the first on the field.___ But my son can't en-joy play-ing ball, not my boy, he's con-

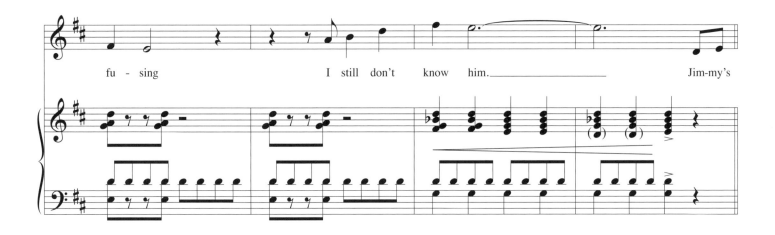

fu - sing I still don't know him._____ Jim-my's

al - most there___ but he's al-most not.___ Like a name you knew___ and then soon for-got.___ Jim-my's

Pedal OK

al-most lost___ in a made-up world_ and I wish he would lis - ten to rea - son.___ Jim-my's

I pushed my dreams to the side. Got my kids got my wife, my a-

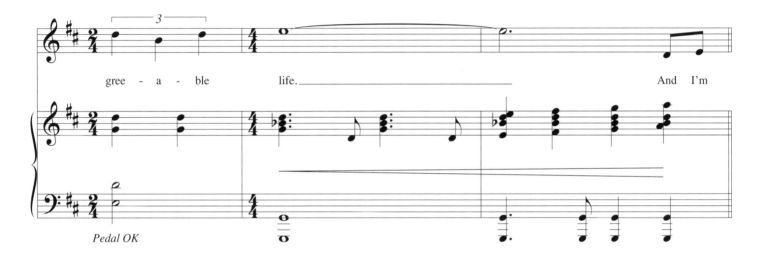

gree - a - ble life._____ And I'm

Pedal OK

al - most there___ though I al - most fail.___ I can breathe it in___ but I

don't ex - hale.___ He's a boy who needs what I can't sup - ply___ so I

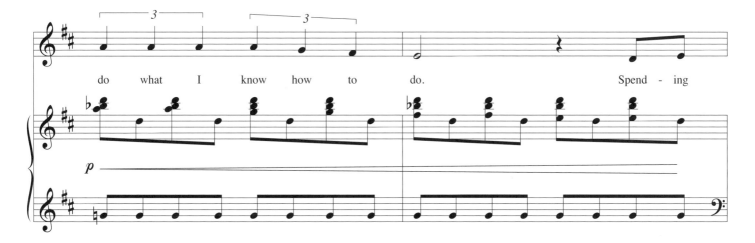

do what I know how to do. Spend - ing

al - most time,_ be - ing al - most where,_ do - ing al - most not,_ giv - ing

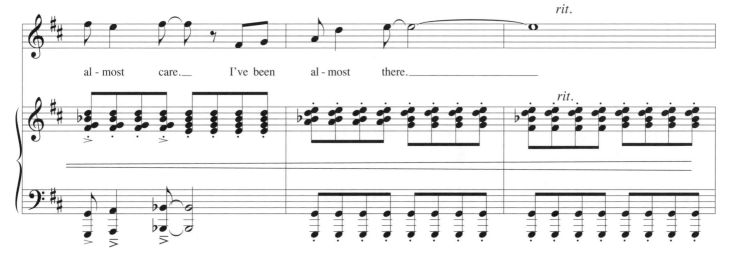

al - most care._ I've been al - most there._____

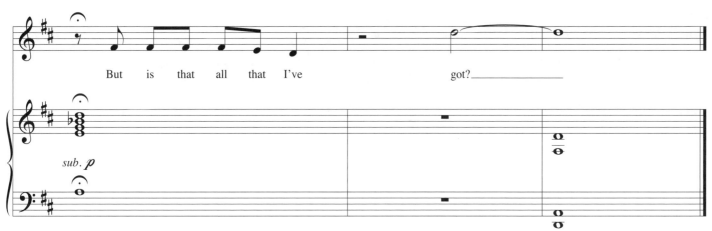

But is that all that I've got?_____

HANDS

Words and Music by
ANDREW LIPPA

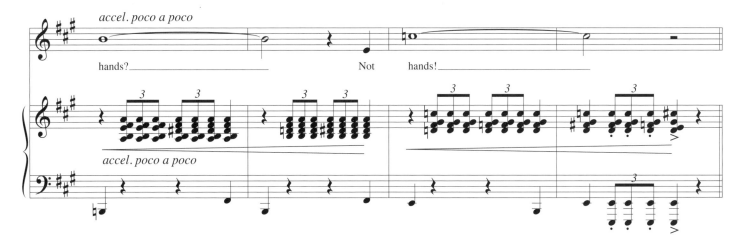

Più Mosso, March Like ♩ = 125

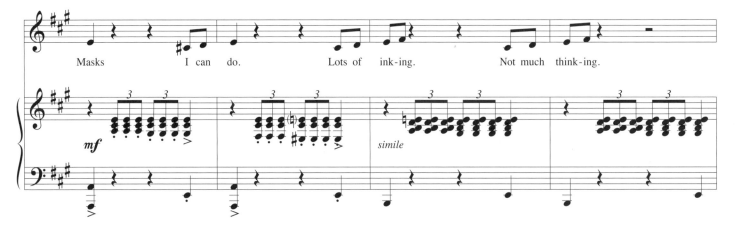

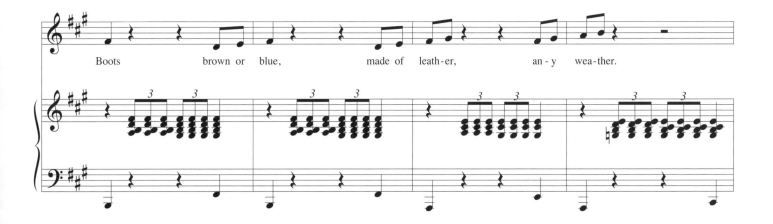

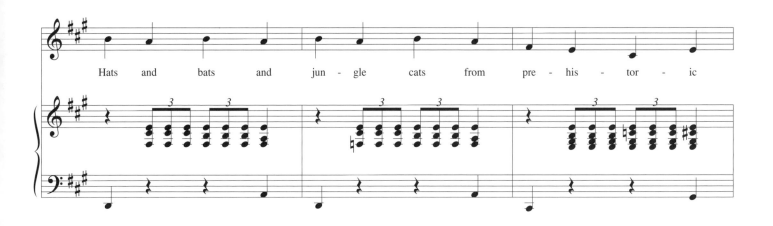

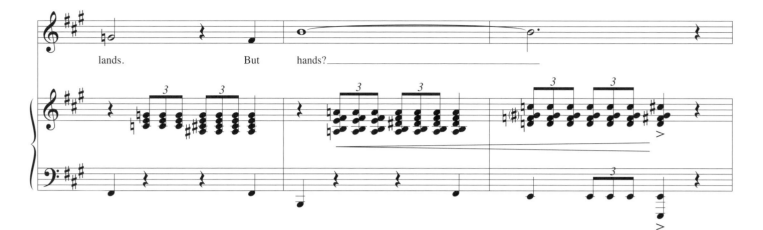

lands.   But   hands?

Who's up - set   by   su - per - he - roes   fly - ing   with their   fin - gers   in   their   pock - ets?____   Would

an - y - bod - y   cry?   Who would   no - tice   when that   su - per   he - ro's   some - where   up   there   in   the

sky?   Not   I!   Heads   I   can

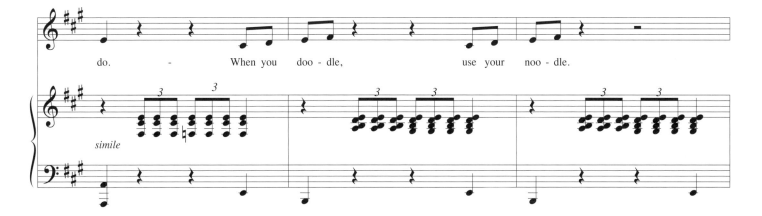

do. - When you doo-dle, use your noo-dle.

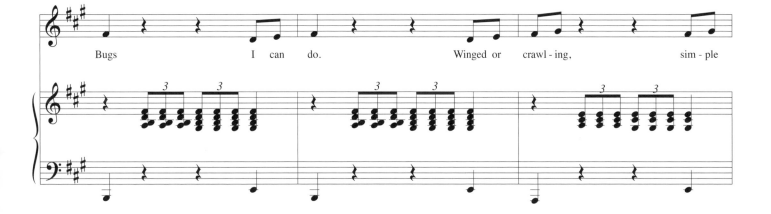

Bugs I can do. Winged or crawl-ing, sim-ple

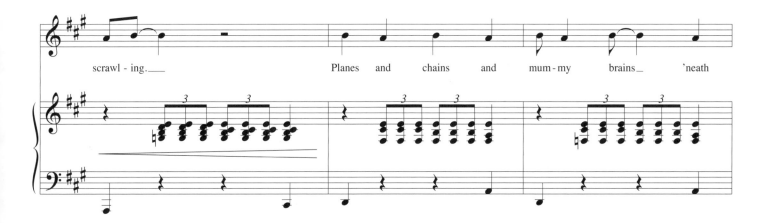

scrawl-ing. Planes and chains and mum-my brains 'neath

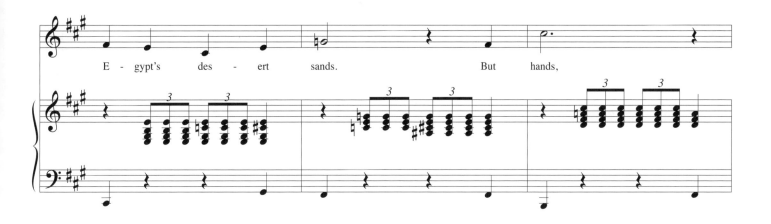

E-gypt's des-ert sands. But hands,

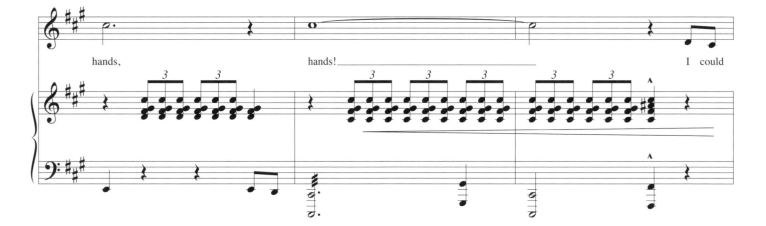

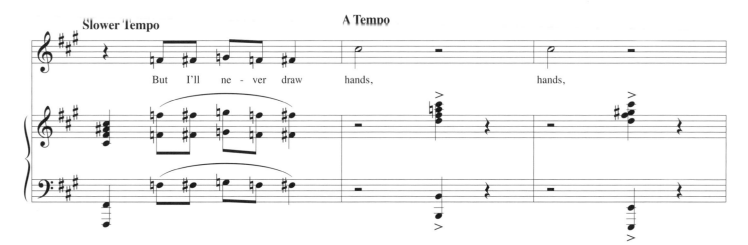

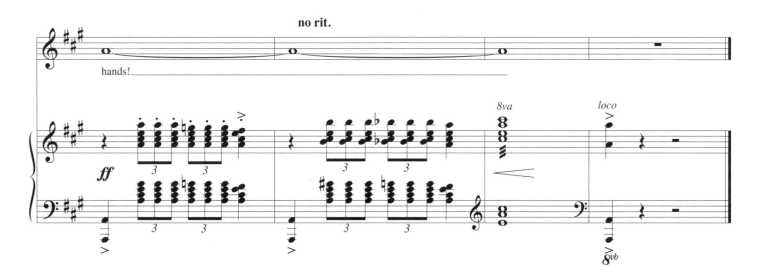

DISAPPEAR

Words and Music by
ANDREW LIPPA

Constant 8th Notes ♩ = 90

NOTE: *Vocal is as free as possible.*

MOTHER:
Ev-'ry day I go to work, I show up where and when I am ex - pec-ted. I like the chal-lenge.

Col-ors, fab-rics, shapes, I get to play with them and see what might be born. It's quite a chal-lenge.

Cli - ents trust my judg-ment, I as-sure them. Pay me for my judg - ment, I a-dore them.

poco rit.   *a tempo*

I can dis - ap - pear   once   more.

FATHER:

Feel-ing like a stran-ger in a home that's grow-ing strang-er by the   ho - ur.___   She seems un-bal-anced.

One by one, the peo-ple in this   house are grow-ing hard-er to ac - cept.

Dis - ap - pear.   Should I   dis - ap - pear?   Should I

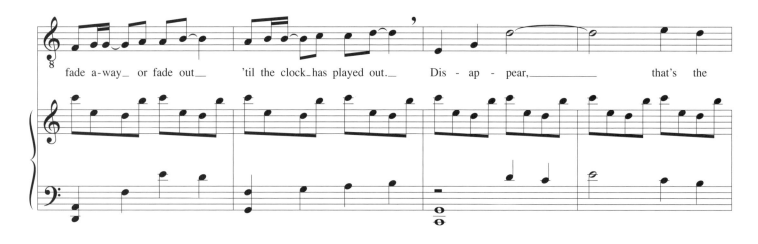

fade a-way_ or fade out_ 'til the clock_has played out._ Dis - ap - pear,_____ that's the

sign they give. Though I try to be a fa-ther and_ make do, I

seem to dis - ap - pear on cue.

MOTHER: Do I dis-en-gage? Do I o-ver - think? How I wish he

FATHER: Do I dis-ap-point? Do I o-ver-look? I don't know what I should know.

speak to you.

speak to you.

a tempo

Ev-'ry day I go to work, I show up where and when I am ex pec - ted.

a tempo

Dis - ap - pear._____ Should I dis - ap - pear?_____ Should I

f *a tempo*

poco rit.

Co-lors, fab-rics, shapes, I get to play with them and see what might be born. That's the

poco rit.

fade a - way or fade out__ 'til the clock has played out?__ Dis - ap - pear_____ that's the

poco rit.

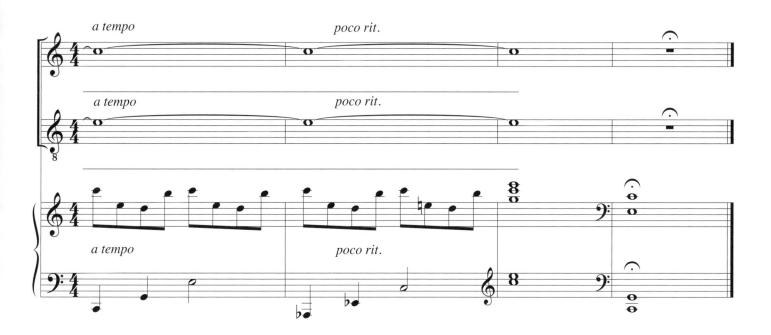

MAYBE HE LIKES ME

Words and Music by
ANDREW LIPPA

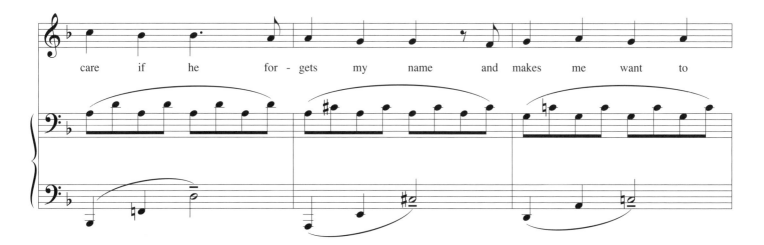

care if he for-gets my name and makes me want to

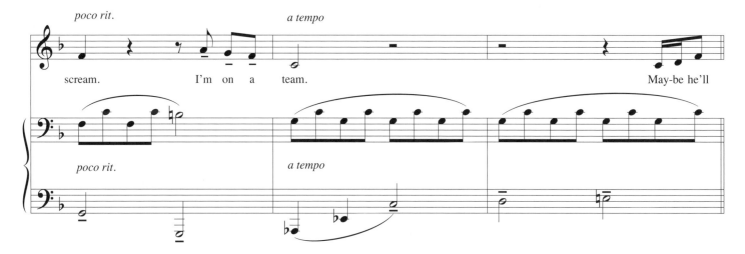

poco rit. scream. *a tempo* I'm on a team. May-be he'll

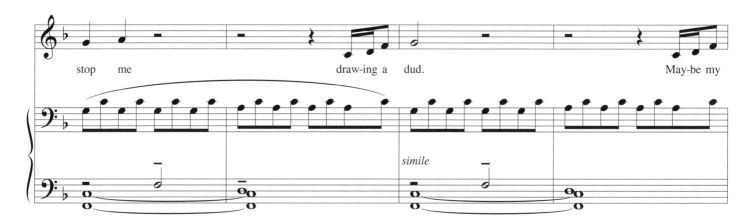

stop me draw-ing a dud. May-be my

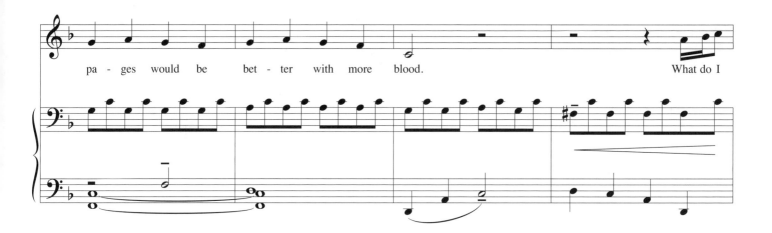

pa-ges would be bet-ter with more blood. What do I

care if he ac - cu - ses me of be - ing much too slow. I think he

likes me and that's all I need to know.

How, Char - ley? Help me through it.

See your great i - de - as to the end.

win his praise, who knows? May-be my dad might e - ven play with me... May - be he

likes me. May-be that's stu-pid.

I can draw it, Char - ley. Please, like my

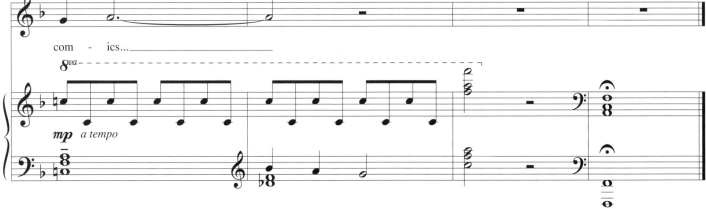

com - ics...

KIDDING AROUND

Words and Music by
ANDREW LIPPA

34

The Fattest Half-Time You've Ever Felt

-ber the fun__ that we had.__ But I can't__ break my word. to my dad.__

sub. p   f

As Before

Kid-ding a-round, no more kid-ding a-round.

mf

I'm gon-na grow. up in-stead._____ Sud-den-ly found, I'm not

Back In Half

kid-ding a-round,__ so get in,__ and get in,__ and get in,__ and get in,__ and get in,__

and get in,___ and get in,___ and get in,___ and get in,___

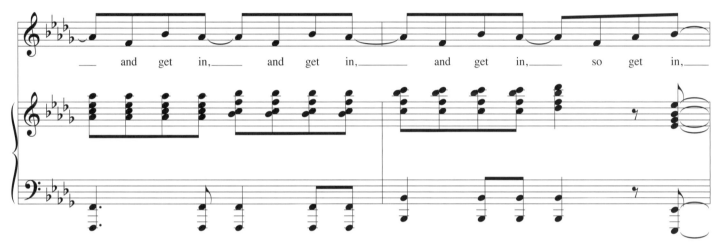

and get in,___ and get in,___ and get in,___ so get in,___

As Before

and get un - der the bed!___

WHERE IS MY LOVE SONG?

Words and Music by
ANDREW LIPPA

One day-to go, I'll make it so right here, right now.____

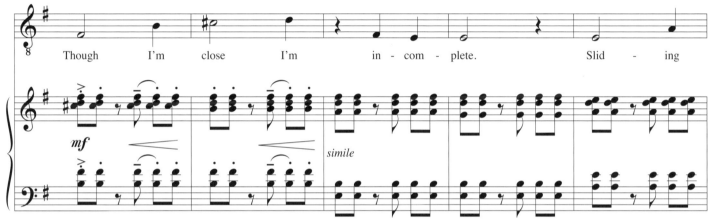

Though I'm close I'm in - com - plete. Slid - ing

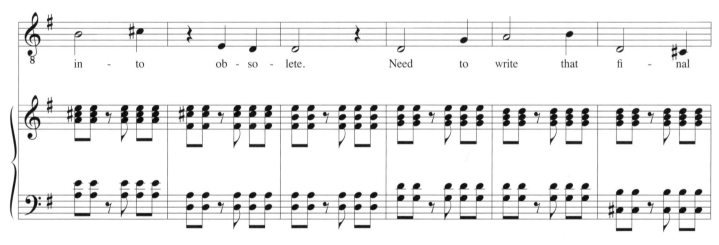

in - to ob - so - lete. Need to write that fi - nal

Don't Rush!

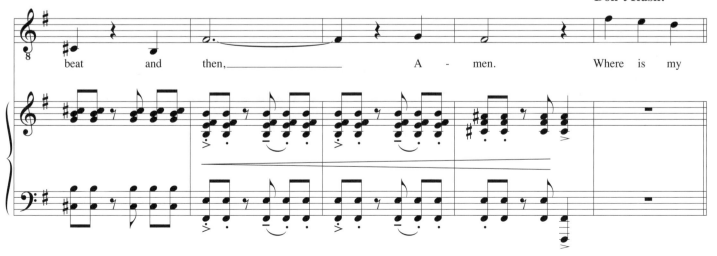

beat and then,_____ A - men. Where is my

40

FATHER: "D-minus in English. Drawing in the margins of his text books. F in History."

FATHER:

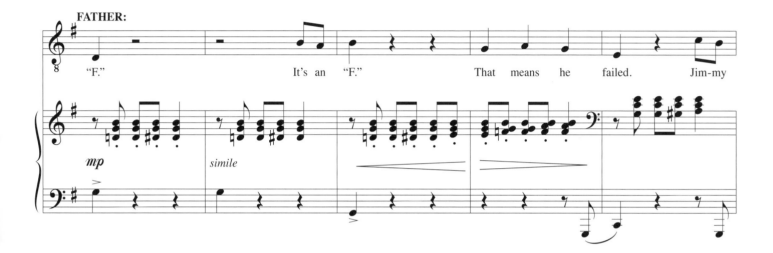

"F." It's an "F." That means he failed. Jim-my

failed on the In - ca test. Clear - ly, his head's out in

space now.____ But this is the prob - lem we face now.____

42

46

48

A Touch Faster

HORRORHEAD & LIGHTNING LADY:

Jim - my, don't ig - nore us. Jim - my, we're your cho - rus.

INCA BINCA & WINMAN:
TOLEDO JACKSON:

Jim - my, don't ig - nore us. Jim - my, we're your cho - rus.

Jim - my, can you please do this one thing for us? Don't give

Jim - my, can you please do this one thing for us? Don't give

up on the things you love, Jim - my, the things you love, Jim - my, you

up on the things you love, Jim - my, the things you love, Jim - my, you

50

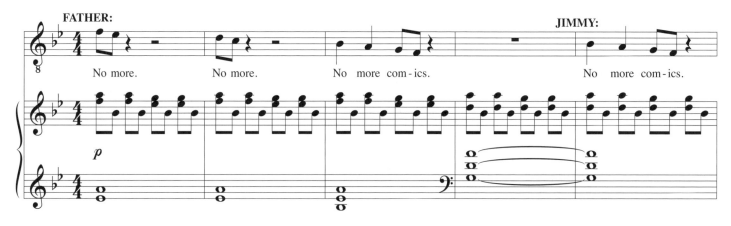

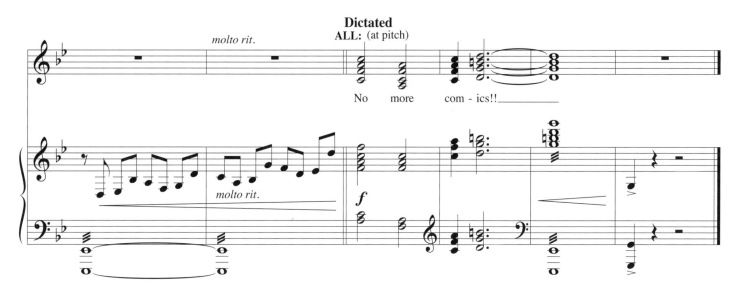

LIKE YOUR SON

Words and Music by
ANDREW LIPPA

Ebb And Flow

MOTHER:
An-tho-ny who lives next door___ has two boys. Both of them, ath-let-ic,

un-a-pol-o-get-ic. Sat-ur-days_ they load_ the car_ with all the base-ball gear_ and oh,___

Simple ♩ = 82

___ they dis-ap-pear.___ But your___ boy makes_ no sense___

___ him.___ To give___ him time___ and space._____ If you'd on-ly pro-tect_

___ him_____ then, he___ might find___ his place._____ But, in-stead,_ you re-ject_

As Before

___ him___ when you___should, face___ to face,_____ say, "I'm proud of you."_____

Were you like___ your son?_

Pas-sion-ate__ and lost.__ Some-one like your son, who'd reach his goal at an-y cost.__

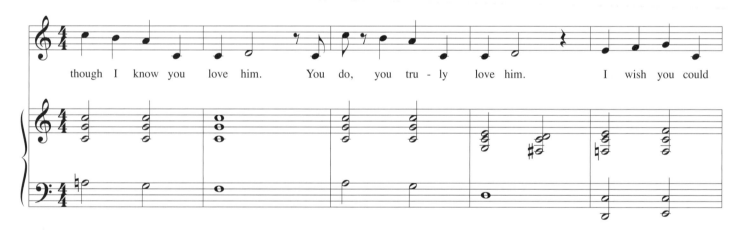

_____ Les-ter's like your son. That's why you turn and run... And

though I know you love him. You do, you tru-ly love him. I wish you could

Più Mosso

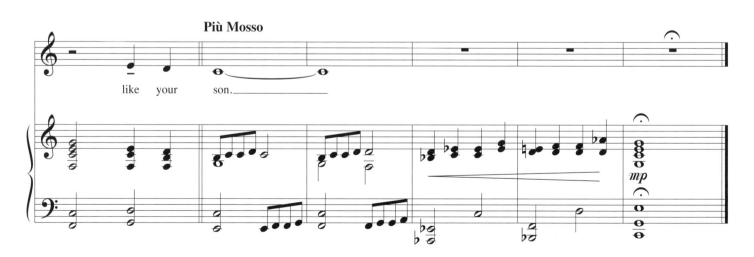

like your son.__

DRAW YOUR OWN CONCLUSION

Words and Music by
ANDREW LIPPA

*NOTE: This can be performed as a solo version if preferred.

_____ to fall,_ to fail.___ May - be you_ can help___ me now,

e - ven if___ you don't___ know how._ **MOTHER:** Draw your own_ con-clu - sion.

Build your own_ es-cape._ Wrap your-self in poss - i - ble__ and watch your life_ take shape._

Chart your own_ di-rec - tion. Choose what's right for you.__ Draw your own_ con-clu - sion and all_

Tempo 1 ♩ = 88

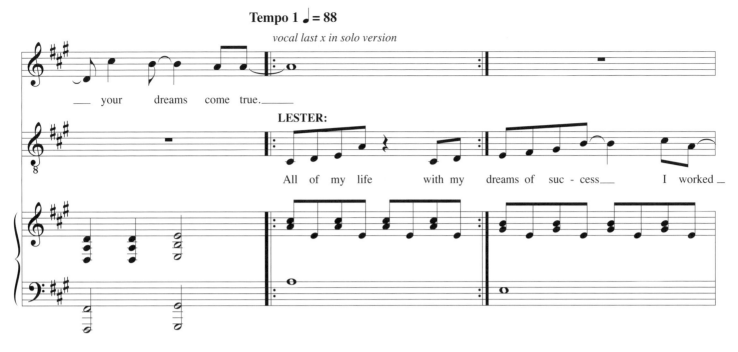

vocal last x in solo version

___ your dreams come true.___

LESTER:

All of my life with my dreams of suc - cess___ I worked ___

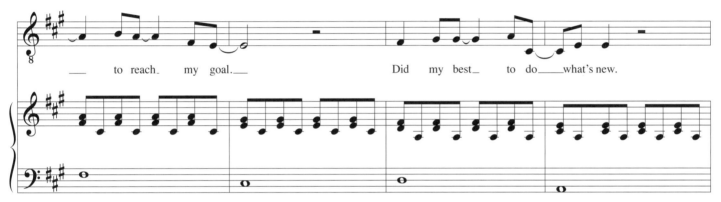

___ to reach___ my goal.___ Did my best___ to do___what's new.

Hoped that you___ would do___ it too._____

JIMMY:

Draw your own___ con-clu - sion. Make your own___ mis-takes.___ Don't give up and don't give in___ and

mf

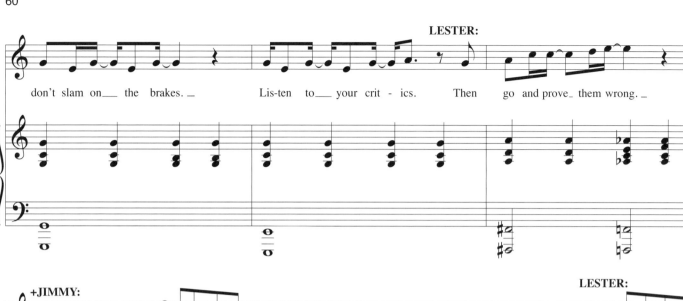

don't slam on___ the brakes. ___ Lis-ten to___ your crit - ics. Then go and prove___ them wrong. ___

Draw your own___ con-clu - sion and you___ can sing___ your song._____ I ran out of

strength and out___ of hope.___ You reached out a hand and drew___ a rope.___ I thought I was

done with art,___ it's true.___ But let's keep do-ing what we do.

Choose what's right for you.___ Draw your own___ con - clu - sion._____

Choose what's right for you.___ Draw your own___ con - clu - sion._____

___ Draw your own___ con - clu - sion_____

___ Draw your own___ con - clu - sion_____

and you can sing your

and you can sing your

song._____ Sing your

song._____ Sing your

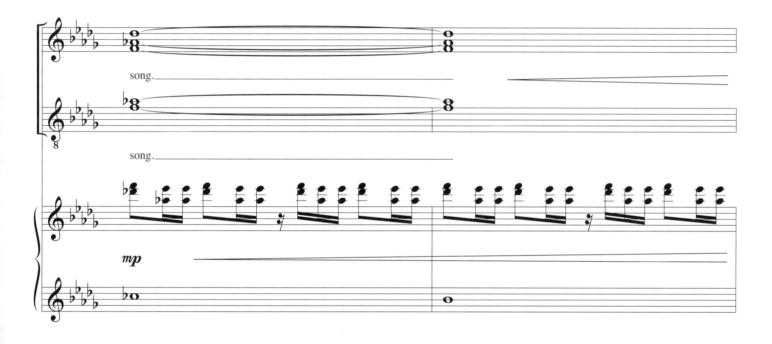

song._____

song._____

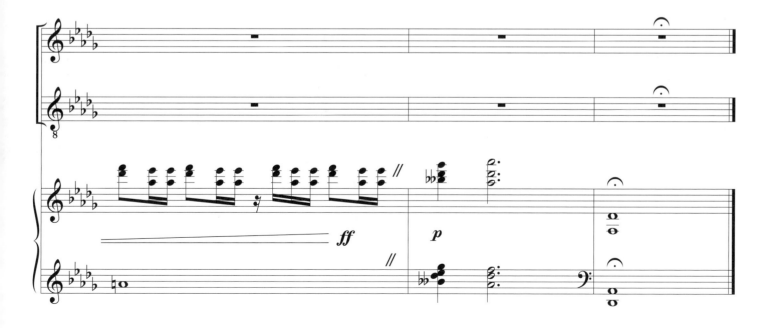

I DO WHAT I DO

Words and Music by
ANDREW LIPPA

do what I do___ be it old,___ be it new,___ that's not___ for me to say.___ I

do what I do___ 'cuz I like___ what I do___ and I love___ my life this

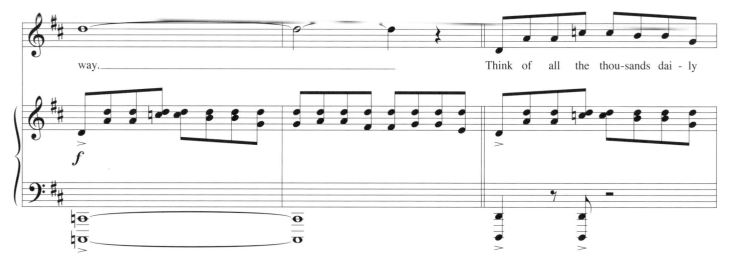

way.___ Think of all the thou-sands dai - ly

la - bor - ing to make their voice o - rig - i - nal. It's eas - ier said than done.

do what I do 'cuz I like what I do and I do,___ do, do___ like you.___ And if

you like graph - ic nov - els,___ I'll be prompt - ly graph - ic, too.___ I

do what I do,___ for a lot,___ for a few,_ let For - tune bring_ what may.___ I

do what I do,___ let 'em cheer,___ let 'em boo!__ I still love___ my life—

Do I look like the guy__ who fix-es cars? I'm more the kind__ who walks a - mong the stars. So I've-

never scored a goal,__ can't fix the o - zone hole,__ won't win the Su - per-bowl__ or land on Mars. But

Soaring

I know a thing or two__ 'bout make - be - liev-ing.__ Some say it's mag-i - cal,__ some self - de - ceiv-ing... Still, I

Much Slower - Ad Lib Tempo

do what I do__ ev - 'ry day a de - but,__ a treas - ure yet to find.__

Let them tear my work_ to piec - es, I still

Big Build   *accel.*

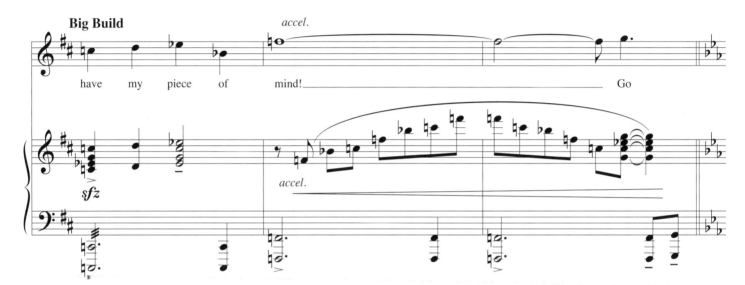

have my piece of mind!_____ Go

a tempo

do what you do   and as long___ as it's true,_ pur - sue___ with all___ your might.___ May-be

what you draw_ this morn - ing___ will be price - less by to - night.___ Yes,

TO THE GODS

Words and Music by
ANDREW LIPPA

* All of Father's pitches are notated an octave higher that sounding unless otherwise directed.

dreams come true. From the God of Broad - way mu - si - cals_

A Bit Brighter

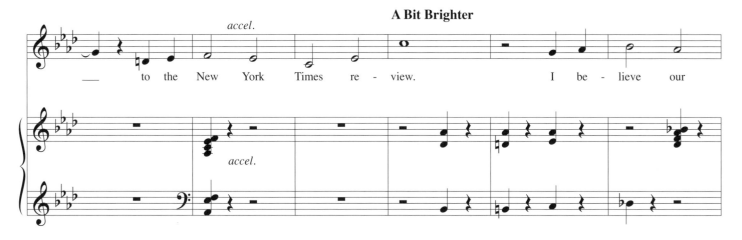

accel.

_ to the New York Times re - view. I be - lieve our

accel.

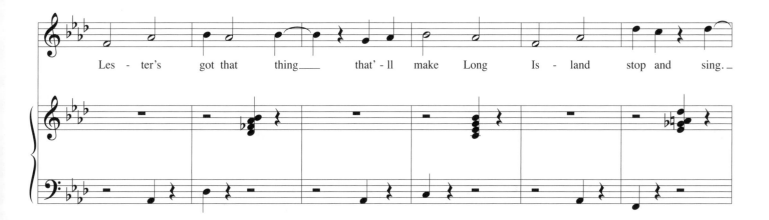

Les - ter's got that thing_ that' - ll make Long Is - land stop and sing._

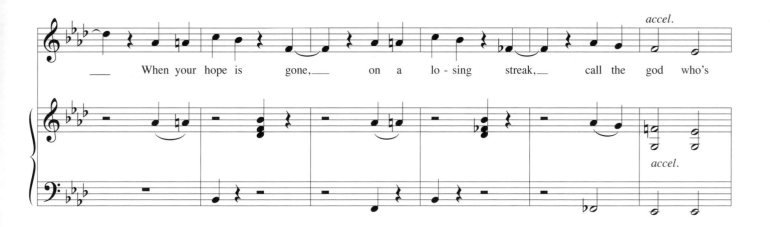

accel.

_ When your hope is gone,_ on a lo - sing streak,_ call the god who's

accel.

74

A Tempo - Brighter, Showbiz 2

counts the roy - al - ties.___ You're a show - biz god,___ so I'll knock on wood.

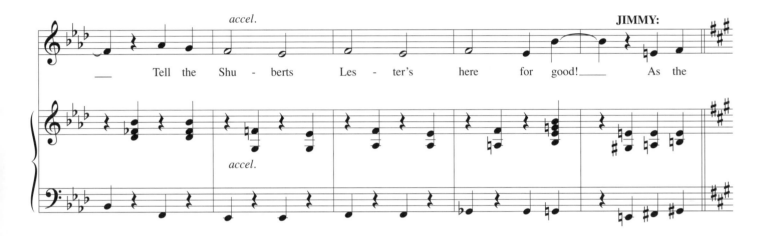

___ Tell the Shu - berts Les - ter's here for good!___ As the

god of Broad - way mu - si - cals,___ we ex - pect a lit - tle

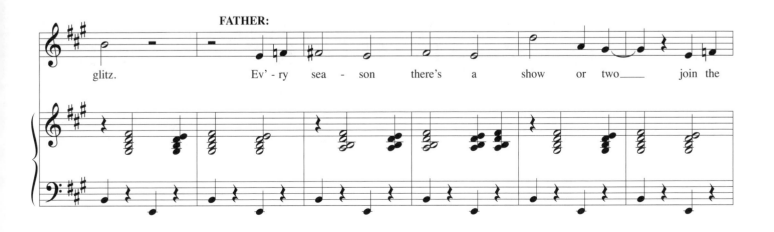

glitz. Ev' - ry sea - son there's a show or two___ join the

78

went to Jui - lli - ard.____ But the one we want,____ and we

____ to Jui - lli - ard.____ But the one we want,____ and we

Big Pullback!

ALL 4:

all a - gree,____ is the god who reads Va - ri - e - ty!____

Ev - 'ry-one reads Va - ri - e - ty! So the